DAY HIKES IN THE
GRAND TETONS
&
JACKSON HOLE
WYOMING

by Robert Stone

D1314522

Photographs by Robert Stone
Published by:
Day Hike Books, Inc.
114 South Hauser Box 865
Red Lodge, MT 59068
Copyright 1996
Library of Congress Catalog Card Number: 95-92665

Distributed by:
ICS Books, Inc.
1370 E. 86th Place
Merrillville, IN 46410
1-800-541-7323
Fax 1-800-336-8334

TABLE OF CONTENTS

THE HIKES
IN GRAND TETON NATIONAL PARK

THE HIKES
IN AND AROUND JACKSON HOLE

About the Hikes

The Day Hikes guide to the Grand Tetons and Jackson Hole focuses on scenic day hikes of various lengths. All of the hikes are inside Grand Teton National Park and around the Jackson Hole area in Wyoming. My goal is to share these hikes with you and others, providing visitors as well as locals easy access to the backcountry. Although the national park is known for its great hikes and more than 200 miles of well-maintained trails, people are often surprised to discover how many wonderful nature hikes are to be found outside the park. The hikes around Jackson Hole are equally beautiful but less crowded.

Jackson Hole is an area 40 miles long running north and south along the Teton Range. This 10-mile wide valley is defined on its west by the majestic Teton Mountains. This rugged range of mountains boasts 10 peaks rising above 12,000 feet and is covered with glaciers, morainal lakes, and precipitous canyons. The centerpiece of the 96,000-acre Grand Teton National Park is the three snowcapped Teton peaks of Teewinot, Grand Teton, and Mount Owen, known collectively as the Cathedral Group. These peaks rise 7000 feet from the valley floor to a high of 13,770 feet at the summit of Grand Teton.

At the base of these mountains is a string of lakes, including Taggart, Bradley, Jenny, String, Leigh, and Jackson. The 25,500-acre Jackson Lake is fed by the Snake River. The Snake River, Wyoming's largest river, winds through Jackson Hole, past the Tetons, and south through the town of Jackson. It plays host to scenic float trips, whitewater rafting, canoeing, and kayaking.

There is abundant wildlife throughout the Jackson Hole area, including grizzly and black bear, moose, bison, elk, antelope, deer, coyote, trumpeter swan, osprey, and eagles. To the north of Jackson is the 25,000-acre National Elk Refuge. Thousands of elk descend each winter to this site.

The major access roads to the hikes in this book are Highway 89, which runs north and south along the Grand Tetons through Jackson Hole; Teton Park Road, which runs through the Park; and Highway 22, heading northwest out of Jackson towards Idaho. Each of these hikes is detailed on United States Geological Survey topo maps listed with the hikes and can be purchased at most area sporting goods stores. The elevations of these hikes are all between 6000 and 8000 feet.

All of the hikes listed in this guide require easy to moderate effort and are timed at a leisurely rate. If you wish to hike faster or go further, set your own pace accordingly. As I hike, I enjoy looking at clouds, rocks, wildflowers, streams, vistas, and any other subtle pleasures of nature. While this adds to the time, it also adds to the experience.

As for attire and equipment, tennis shoes, as opposed to hiking boots, are fine for any of these hikes. A rain poncho, sunscreen, and mosquito repellent are recommended. Drinking water is a must. Pack a lunch for a picnic at scenic overlooks, streams, or wherever you find the best spot.

Enjoy your hike!

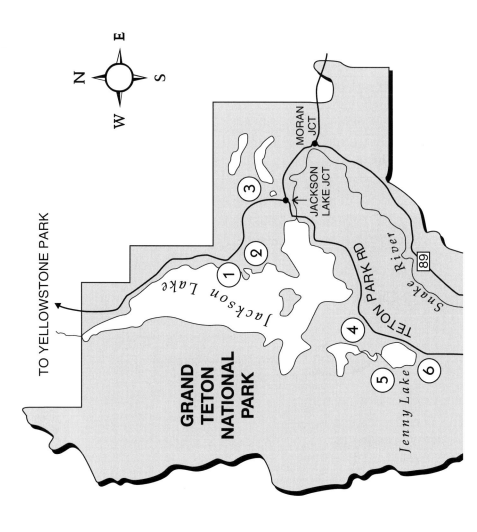

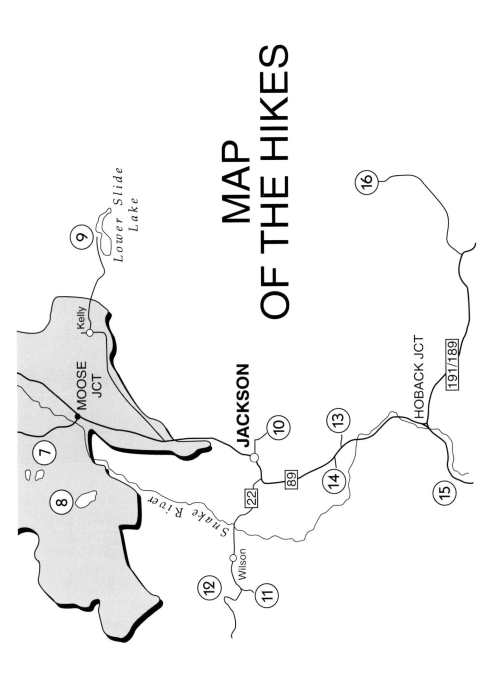

MAP
OF THE HIKES

Hike 1
Lakeshore Trail at Colter Bay

Hiking distance: 2 miles round trip
Hiking time: 1 hour
Elevation gain: Level hiking
Topo: U.S.G.S. Colter Bay
　　　　Trails Illustrated Grand Teton National Park

Summary of hike: This is an exceptional hike for water lovers. The trail follows a section of shoreline along Colter Bay and Jackson Lake. It crosses a causeway and circles a peninsula protruding into Jackson Lake. Throughout the hike, there are exceptional views of the Teton Mountain Range and the 25,000-acre Jackson Lake.

Driving directions: From downtown Jackson, drive 12.3 miles north on Highway 89 towards Grand Teton National Park to Teton Park Road and turn left. A short distance ahead is the national park entrance. Continue 25 miles to the Colter Bay Road and turn left. One mile ahead, at the end of the road, is the Colter Bay Visitor Center parking lot.

Hiking directions: From the parking lot, walk behind the visitor center to the shoreline. Follow the paved trail left along the north shore of the marina through the lodgepole pine trees. At 0.5 miles is a sign marking the "Lakeshore Foot Trail" junction—go right. Shortly ahead, you will cross a causeway which separates Jackson Lake and Colter Bay. Follow the trail to the left which circles the perimeter of the peninsula in a clockwise direction. The beach at the far end of the peninsula is a wonderful area for a picnic. The trail continues along the shoreline back to the causeway. After crossing, take the trail to the left, following the shoreline of Jackson Lake back to the Colter Bay parking lot.

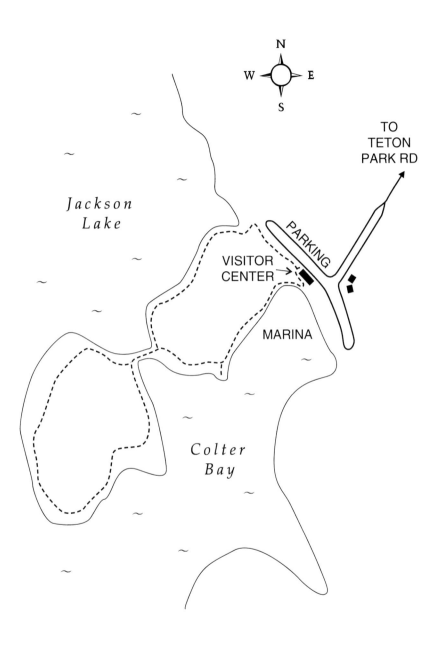

N
W E
S

TO
TETON
PARK RD

PARKING

Jackson
Lake

VISITOR
CENTER

MARINA

Colter
Bay

LAKESHORE TRAIL

Hike 2
Swan Lake and Heron Pond

Hiking distance: 3 miles round trip
Hiking time: 1.5 hours
Elevation gain: Level hiking
Topo: U.S.G.S. Colter Bay
            Trails Illustrated Grand Teton National Park

Summary of hike: Along the pristine trail to Heron Pond and Swan Lake are stands of lodgepole pines and the ever-present Teton peaks. Both the pond and the lake have abundant water lilies and water fowl, including pelicans, osprey, trumpeter swan, cranes, heron, Canada geese, and ducks. Moose and elk are frequently spotted in this area. This 3-mile loop is the beginning of the 9-mile loop to Hermitage Point, a popular full-day hike.

Driving directions: From downtown Jackson, drive 12.3 miles north on Highway 89 towards Grand Teton National Park to Teton Park Road and turn left. A short distance ahead is the national park entrance. Continue 25 miles to the Colter Bay Road and turn left. One mile ahead, at the end of the road, is the Colter Bay Visitor Center parking lot.

Hiking directions: The trailhead is on the south end of the parking lot by the marina boat launch. Take the "Hermitage Point Foot Trail" to the right along the Colter Bay shoreline. There is a trail junction at 0.4 miles. Take the trail to the right, towards Heron Pond, staying close to the shoreline. At one mile, you will reach the north end of Heron Pond. The trail continues along the east shore of the pond to another trail junction 0.4 miles further. Our hike follows the left trail, which loops back towards Swan Lake. (The trail to the right leads south to Hermitage point.) The trail heads north and runs along the west shore of Swan Lake. A short distance ahead, the trail curves left, completing the loop, and returns to the Colter Bay parking lot.

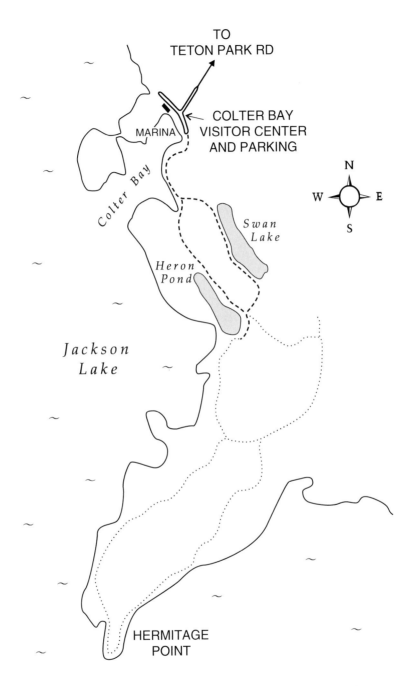

TO
TETON PARK RD

COLTER BAY
VISITOR CENTER
AND PARKING

MARINA

Colter Bay

Swan Lake

Heron Pond

Jackson Lake

N
W   E
S

HERMITAGE
POINT

SWAN LAKE & HERON POND

Hike 3
Christian Pond Trail

Hiking distance: 3.2 miles round trip
Hiking time: 1.5 hours
Elevation gain: Level with rolling hills
Topo: U.S.G.S. Moran and Two Ocean Lake
Trails Illustrated Grand Teton National Park

Summary of hike: This hike circles around Christian Pond, a waterfowl habitat and nesting area for trumpeter swan. The rolling hills in this area are covered in sage and stands of lodgepole pines. Open meadows offer commanding views of the Teton Mountains. Bring your binoculars for bird watching and possible moose observation.

Driving directions: From downtown Jackson, drive 12.3 miles north on Highway 89 towards Grand Teton National Park to Teton Park Road and turn left. A short distance ahead is the national park entrance. Continue 21 miles, passing Jackson Lake Junction, to Jackson Lodge Road. Turn left. Drive 0.2 miles and turn left again towards the corrals. Park in the first parking area on the right.

Hiking directions: From the parking lot, follow the trail east, passing the horse corrals towards the highway bridge. The trail dips and crosses under the bridge to a signed trail junction. Take the trail to the right 0.3 miles to the Christian Pond Overlook. After enjoying this area, continue 0.3 miles to another signed trail junction. Take the trail to the left, which reads "via Emma Matilda Lake." Along this portion of the trail, there are several unmarked Y-junctions. Stay left at each one. By staying left, you will loop around Christian Pond, returning to the highway bridge. Cross back under the bridge to the corrals and parking lot.

If you wish to enjoy a longer hike, trails lead to both Emma Matilda Lake and Two Ocean Lake after the Christian Pond Overlook. Take the trails to the right at the signed junctions.

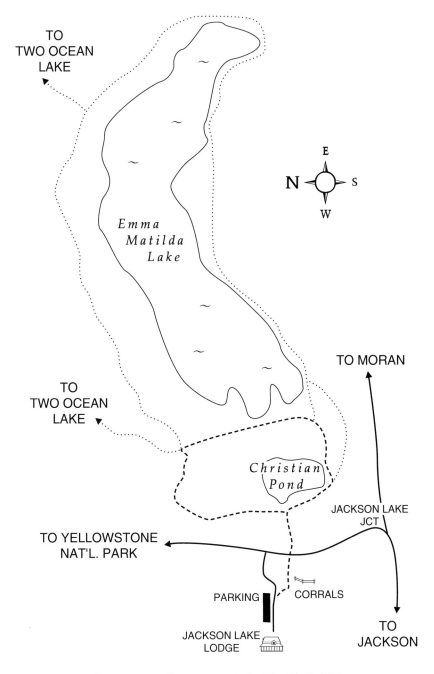

TO
TWO OCEAN
LAKE

E
N · S
W

Emma
Matilda
Lake

TO MORAN

TO
TWO OCEAN
LAKE

Christian
Pond

JACKSON LAKE
JCT

TO YELLOWSTONE
NAT'L. PARK

PARKING   CORRALS

JACKSON LAKE
LODGE

TO
JACKSON

CHRISTIAN POND

Hike 4
String and Leigh Lakes Trail

Hiking Distance: 4.4 to 7.4 miles round trip
Hiking Time: 2 to 3.5 hours
Elevation Gain: Level hiking
Topo: U.S.G.S. Jenny Lake
           Trails Illustrated Grand Teton National Park

Summary of hike: Both String Lake and Leigh Lake have magnificent views of the Cathedral Group—the three Teton peaks of Teewinot, Grand Teton, and Mount Owen. This hike strolls along the eastern shore of both lakes. These are popular lakes for swimming and canoeing. The narrow String Lake connects Leigh Lake to Jenny Lake.

Driving directions: From downtown Jackson, drive 12.3 miles north on Highway 89 towards Grand Teton National Park to Teton Park Road and turn left. One mile ahead is the national park entrance. From this entrance continue 10.2 miles to the North Jenny Lake Junction and turn left. Drive 0.9 miles to the String Lake picnic area and turn right. Park a short distance ahead in the parking lot.

Hiking directions: From the parking lot, several asphalt walking paths will lead to the trailhead at String Lake. This trail closely follows the shore of String Lake for 0.9 miles to the south tip of Leigh Lake. There are two trail junctions within 300 feet of each other. Take the right fork both times, staying on the Leigh Lake Trail. The trail continues north along the east shore. At 2.2 miles is the sandy East Shore Beach. Although the trail continues 1.5 miles further to Bearpaw Lake, this beach is our turn around spot. To return, follow the same trail back to the parking lot.

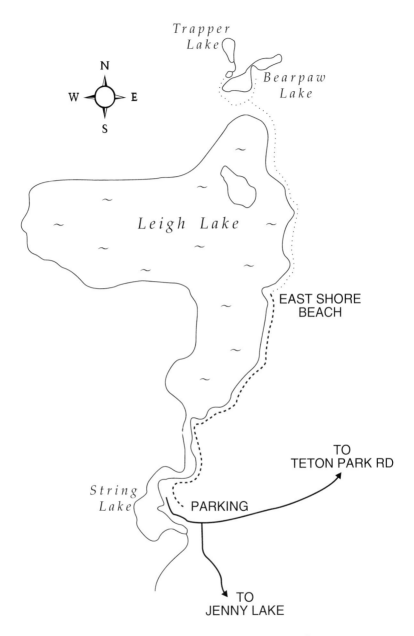

STRING AND LEIGH LAKES TRAIL

Hike 5
Hidden Falls and Inspiration Point

Hiking Distance: Via boat shuttle: 1.8 miles round trip
Boat shuttle leaves every 20 minutes
(8 a.m. – 6 p.m.)
Walk south shore: 5.8 miles round trip
Hiking Time: 1.5 hours
Elevation Gain: 450 feet
Topo: U.S.G.S. Jenny Lake, Trails Illustrated Grand Teton N.P.

Summary of hike: Jenny Lake sits at the base of Cascade Canyon. The hike includes a boat crossing towards this canyon. The trail follows cascading waters to a waterfall via several bridge crossings and overlooks the national park and Jackson. During the hike, the Tetons tower overhead.

Driving directions: From downtown Jackson, drive 12.3 miles north on Highway 89 towards Grand Teton National Park to Teton Park Road and turn left. A short distance ahead is the national park entrance. Continue 7 miles to South Jenny Lake Road and turn left. Park in the lot by the ranger station.

Hiking directions: From the parking lot, follow the trail to the boat dock. There are two ways to get to Hidden Falls and Inspiration Point. My favorite is to take the boat shuttle to the west shore of Jenny Lake. There is a small fee but the boat ride is fun. The ride allows for great photo opportunities and shortens the hike by four miles. If you prefer to hike rather than ride the boat, walk around the south shore of Jenny Lake to Cascade Creek.

From the west shore boat dock, a well-defined trail to the left follows Cascade Creek to a footbridge. Crossing this bridge will lead back two miles to the parking lot and ranger station. Just before the bridge, take the trail to the right towards Hidden Falls (0.2 miles) and Inspiration Point (0.7 miles). The trail crosses two other footbridges en route to Inspiration Point. Just before these bridges is a short side trail to the left for an excellent view of Hidden Falls. At Inspiration Point, the Tetons are over your shoulder while Jenny Lake sits 400 feet below. This spot is a geologic marvel. Return on the same path.

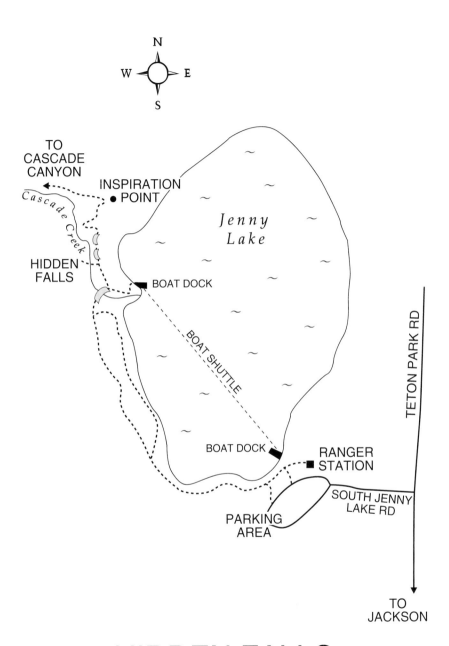

N
W E
S

TO
CASCADE
CANYON

INSPIRATION
● POINT

Cascade Creek

HIDDEN
FALLS

Jenny
Lake

BOAT DOCK

BOAT SHUTTLE

BOAT DOCK

RANGER
STATION

TETON PARK RD

SOUTH JENNY
LAKE RD

PARKING
AREA

TO
JACKSON

HIDDEN FALLS
AND INSPIRATION POINT

Daydreaming at Taggart Lake - Hike 7

View of Tetons at Leigh Lake - Hike 4

Trail by String Lake - Hike 4

On the road to Granite Falls - Hike 16

Hike 6
Jenny Lake Loop

Hiking Distance: Via boat shuttle: 4.5 miles round trip
Boat shuttle leaves every 20 min.
(8 a.m. - 6 p.m.)
Walk south shore: 6.5 miles round trip
Hiking Time: 2.5 hours
Elevation Gain: Level hiking
Topo: U.S.G.S. Jenny Lake
Trails Illustrated Grand Teton National Park

Summary of hike: This is a beautiful hike around the perimeter of the glacial Jenny Lake. Set at the base of the Teton Range, the perimeter of the lake is 6.5 miles. The hike may be shortened two miles by the scenic boat shuttle from the Jenny Lake Ranger Station to the west shore.

Driving directions: From downtown Jackson, drive 12.3 miles north on Highway 89 towards Grand Teton National Park to Teton Park Road and turn left. A short distance ahead is the national park entrance. Continue 7 miles to the South Jenny Lake Road and turn left. Park in the lot by the ranger station.

Hiking directions: From the parking lot, follow the trail to the boat dock. Take the boat shuttle to the west shore of Jenny Lake. There is a small fee for the boat ride. If you prefer to hike rather than ride the boat, walk around the south shore two miles to the bridge crossing Cascade Creek near the west shore dock.
From this boat dock, the well-defined trail heads to the left towards Hidden Falls. Within minutes is a trail junction. Take the right trail which leads around the perimeter of Jenny Lake back to the parking lot and ranger station.

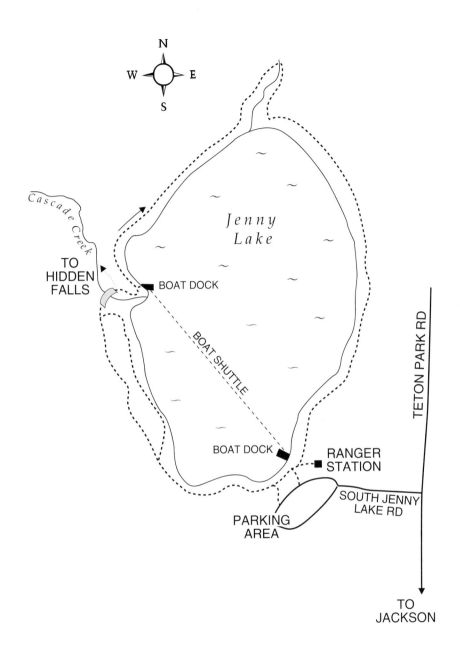

JENNY LAKE LOOP

Bradley Lake and the Tetons - Hike 7

The Teton Peaks from Lower Slide Lake - Hike 9

Views along the trail to Phelps Lake - Hike 8

Phelps Lake - Hike 8

Hike 7
Taggart and Bradley Lakes Loop

Hiking Distance: 4.8 miles round trip
Hiking Time: 3 hours
Elevation Gain: 520 feet
Topo: U.S.G.S. Moose and Grand Teton
         Trails Illustrated Grand Teton National Park

Summary of hike: The glacial lakes of Taggart and Bradley sit at the base of the Teton Range. In 1985, a fire burned the forest around Taggart Lake. The new forest has taken root and is thriving again. The area is green with young aspen and lodgepole trees that blanket the area. On the return, there is an excellent overview of the area as the elevated trail perches over Taggart Lake.

Driving directions: From downtown Jackson, drive 12.3 miles north on Highway 89 towards Grand Teton National Park to Teton Park Road and turn left. One mile ahead is the national park entrance. Continue 2.4 miles to the Taggart Lake Trailhead. Turn left and park.

Hiking directions: From the parking lot, walk west towards the Tetons. At the first trail junction go right. The trail heads uphill and crosses Taggart Creek via footbridges. At 1.1 mile is another well-marked trail junction. This begins the loop portion of the hike. Take the left fork 0.5 miles to Taggart Lake. From here the trail continues to the right along the lake towards Bradley Lake, 1.4 miles ahead. After exploring Bradley Lake, return to the trail junction at the south end of the lake. Take the trail to the left, leaving the lake, and head back 2.1 miles to the parking lot.

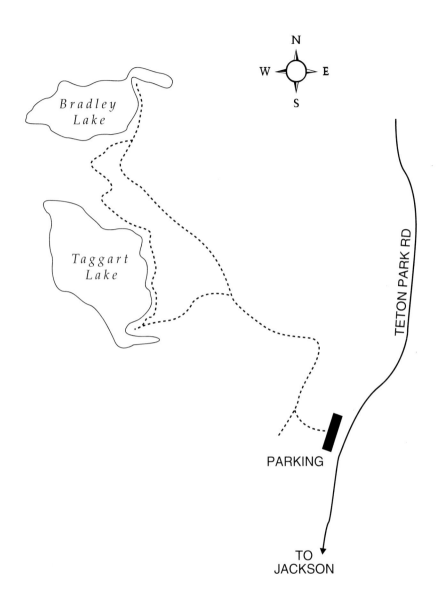

TAGGART AND BRADLEY LAKES LOOP

Hike 8
Phelps Lake

Hiking distance: Phelps Lake Overlook: 2 miles round trip
Phelps Lake: 4 miles round trip
Hiking time: 1 or 2.5 hours
Elevation gain: 600 feet
Topo: U.S.G.S. Grand Teton
Trails Illustrated Grand Teton National Park

Summary of hike: This hike follows a beautifully forested trail to an overlook of the 525-acre Phelps Lake. Along the way are frequent springs and abundant wildflowers. From the overlook we descend to the lake.

Driving directions: From downtown Jackson, drive 12.3 miles north on Highway 89 towards Grand Teton National Park to Teton Park Road and turn left. 0.5 miles ahead is the town of Moose. On the left, across the highway from the Moose Visitor Center, is the Moose-Wilson Road to Teton Village. Turn left and continue 3 miles to the Death Canyon Trailhead turn-off on the right—turn right. 1.6 miles ahead, at the end of the road, is the trailhead parking area.

Hiking directions: From the Death Canyon parking area, the trail is easy to identify. There is a gradual incline to the Phelps Lake Overlook, located 1 mile from the trailhead. The elevation at the overlook is 7200 feet. The trail continues for another mile down the glacial moraine via switchbacks to the western shore of Phelps Lake, which sits at 6600 feet. The turnaround point for this hike is Phelps Lake. To return, retrace your steps.

If you wish to hike further, however, return a short distance in the direction of the Phelps Lake Overlook to the Death Canyon Trail on the left. Follow this trail to the west into Death Canyon. There is a 1000-foot elevation gain into this canyon, making a more strenuous hike. The steep canyon walls and unique rock formations make this hike rewarding. If you hike through the canyon to the meadow by the Death Canyon Patrol Cabin, it will add 3.3 miles round trip to the hiking distance.

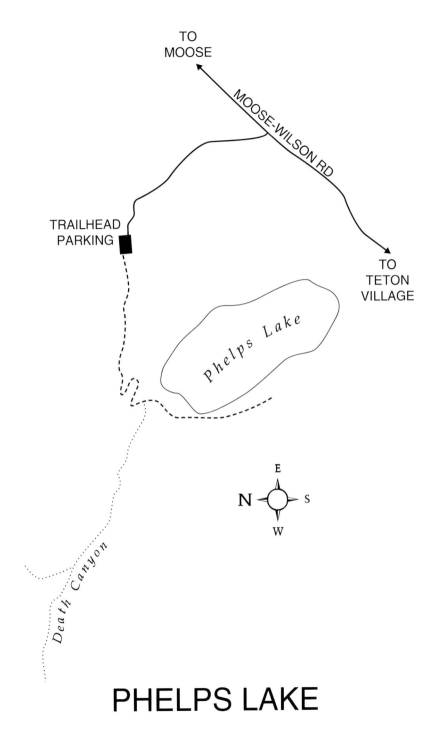

PHELPS LAKE

Hike 9
Gros Ventre
Lower Slide Lake

Hiking Distance: 1.2 miles round trip
Hiking Time: 1 hour
Elevation Gain: 200 feet
Topo: U.S.G.S. Shadow Mountain

Summary of hike: The Gros Ventre Slide Interpretive Trail is a 0.8 mile round trip hike. Signs along the trail teach about the geology of the area, the trees, and the shrubs. This trail has views of the largest natural landslide in North America, which formed a dam across the Gros Ventre River and created Lower Slide Lake. Walking 0.2 miles further leads to this lake.

Driving directions: From Jackson, drive 6.5 miles north on Highway 89 to the Gros Ventre Junction. Turn right at this junction and drive 8 miles to another road junction with the "Gros Ventre Road" sign. Turn right and drive 4.7 miles to the trailhead. The parking turnout is on the right.

Hiking directions: Follow the trail from the parking area. As you hike, other trail options appear. They all weave around and reconnect with the main loop. The Fishermen Trails lead to Lower Slide Lake and are worth exploring. Return on the same trails back to your car.

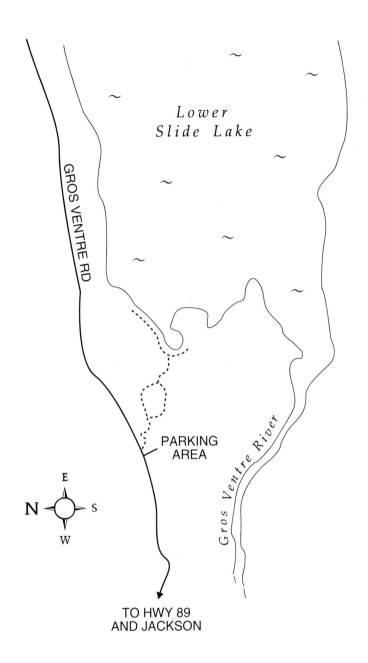

GROS VENTRE
LOWER SLIDE LAKE

Hike 10
Cache Creek Canyon Loop

Hiking Distance: 4 miles round trip
Hiking Time: 2 hours
Elevation Gain: 350 feet
Topo: U.S.G.S. Cache Creek

Summary of hike: This trail is close to downtown Jackson, yet it is a wonderful wilderness hike. The hike follows a trail through the forest alongside Cache Creek. It goes deep into the valley and includes views of the Teton mountain peaks.

Driving directions: Drive east on Broadway (the main street through Jackson) 1/2 mile to Redmond Street, across from St. Johns Hospital. Turn right on Redmond Street, and drive 0.4 miles to Cache Creek Drive. Turn left on Cache Creek Drive and continue 1.2 miles to the parking area.

Hiking directions: Begin the hike at the trailhead, just before the parking area on the south side of the road. Cross the bridge over the stream and follow the trail. At about one mile, you have the option of crossing the stream at a log crossing and returning on the jeep trail or continuing on the same trail farther into the valley. At two miles, there is a Y-fork in the trail. The right fork continues deeper into the canyon and connects to other trails, such as Game Creek (Hike 7) and Granite Falls (Hike 9). To return, take the left fork and cross the creek. This involves getting wet feet. It is invigorating. If you wish to stay dry, there are down logs in both directions of this crossing that can be carefully used as a bridge. After the stream crossing, follow the trail through a meadow to the jeep trail which heads gently downhill back to your car.

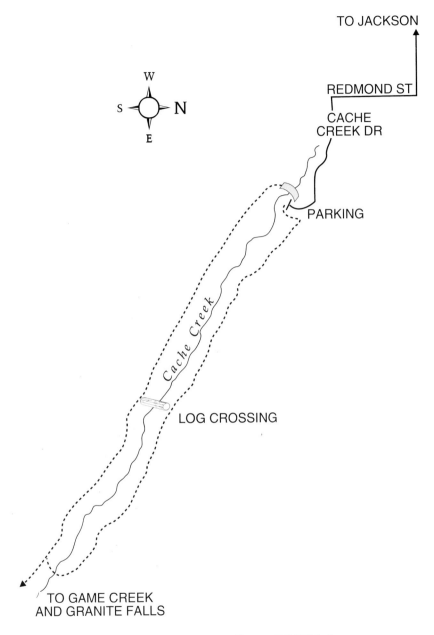

W N S E

TO JACKSON

REDMOND ST

CACHE CREEK DR

PARKING

Cache Creek

LOG CROSSING

TO GAME CREEK
AND GRANITE FALLS

CACHE CREEK
CANYON LOOP

Hike 11
North Fork Creek Loop
to Crater Lake

Hiking Distance: 3 miles round trip
Hiking Time: 1.5 hours
Elevation Gain: 700 feet
Topo: U.S.G.S. Teton Pass

Summary of hike: This trail is a loop which parallels an old abandoned highway and North Fork Creek. This pristine area is covered with an array of wildflowers. The trail leads past a small waterfall and to the shores of a beautiful mountain lake.

Driving directions: From Jackson , head south on Highway 89 a short distance to Highway 22. Turn right and drive toward Wilson. A little over one mile past Wilson is a building on the right side of the road with a large sign that says "Heidelberg"— you can't miss it. Turn left across the highway from this sign. Drive one mile to the end of the road and park.

Hiking directions: Walk around the gate and up the old asphalt road for about 300 yards. Bear to the left onto the hiking trail. This is the beginning of the loop. All along the trail you will hear North Fork Creek below on your left. At one mile, there is a stream crossing with a small but magnificent waterfall. A half mile further, this trail meets the old asphalt road and crosses it to Crater Lake. Cascading water feeds the lake at its north end. Return down the old highway back to your car.

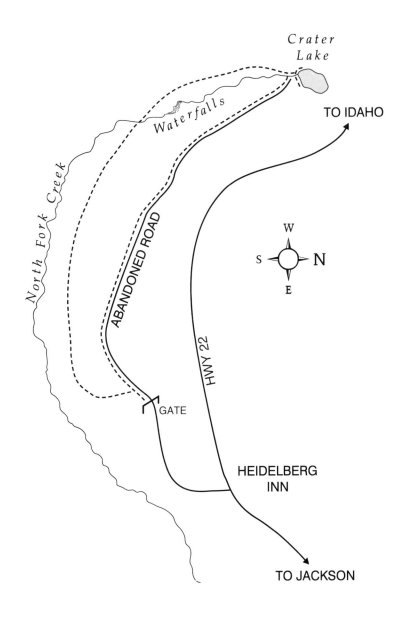

Crater Lake

TO IDAHO

Waterfalls

North Fork Creek

ABANDONED ROAD

HWY 22

W
S ◇ N
E

GATE

HEIDELBERG INN

TO JACKSON

NORTH FORK CREEK
TO CRATER LAKE

Hike 12
Phillips Canyon
and Ski Lake

Hiking Distance: 4 miles round trip
Hiking Time: 2 hours
Elevation Gain: 900 feet
Topo: U.S.G.S. Rendezvous Peak

Summary of hike: This hike leads to a deep blue mountain lake. Along the way, the trail winds through an open meadow bursting with wildflowers. Phillips Canyon opens out into this meadow. The trail winds past Phillips Canyon, crossing a beautiful stream en route to Ski Lake

Driving directions: From Jackson , head south on Highway 89 a short distance to Highway 22. Turn right and drive toward Wilson. Four miles past Wilson, on the right side of the road, is a "Phillips Canyon" trailhead sign. On the left side is a parking area. Turn left and park.

Hiking directions: Walk across the highway to the "Phillips Canyon" sign. Hike up this gravel road about 10 minutes until you reach the trail on the left. There is a Forest Service sign at this trail pointing the way to Ski Lake. The trail is uphill—it is a steady climb but not steep. It soon drops into a beautiful meadow with a stream running through it and lots of wildflowers. After the meadow, the trail follows beside a creek up to Ski Lake. From Ski Lake, take the same trail back to your car.

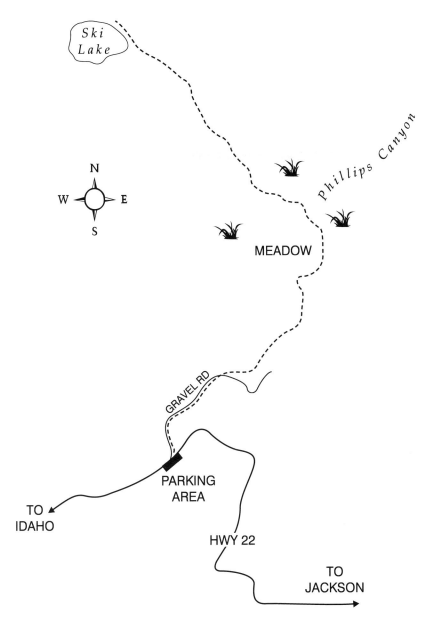

PHILLIPS CANYON
AND SKI LAKE

Hike 13
Game Creek Loop

Hiking Distance: 3 miles round trip
Hiking Time: 1.5 hours
Elevation Gain: 200 feet
Topo: U.S.G.S. Cache Creek

Summary of hike: This hike is a loop with marbled marshland between the trails. The trail follows a beautiful, level valley with wildflowers in abundance and small streams snaking through the meadow.

Driving directions: Drive 7 miles south of Jackson on Highway 89. Between mile markers 146 and 147, turn left on Game Creek Road. Drive 1 mile on asphalt; then bear left onto the jeep trail. (The main road takes a sharp right bend at this gravel turnoff.) Drive 2.2 miles further on the gravel road to the end. At the end is a wooden buck fence and a stream.

Hiking directions: Walk around the buck fence and begin the trail on the left (northwest) side of the valley. Follow the trail as it crosses several small streams. Both trails of this loop meet at a stream crossing by a cattle gate. Return on the hillside trail which overlooks the valley while leading you back to your car.

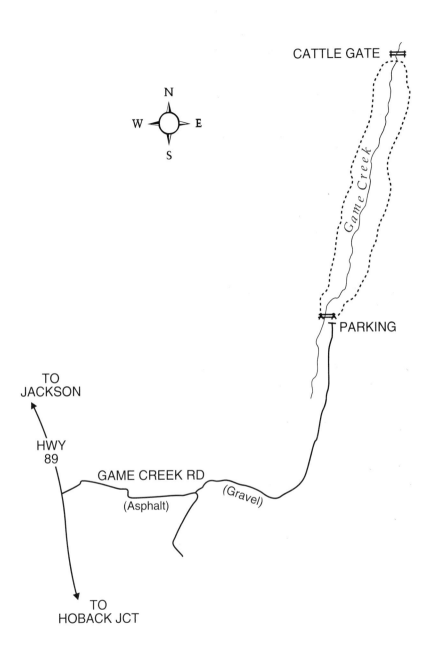

CATTLE GATE

Game Creek

PARKING

TO
JACKSON

HWY
89

GAME CREEK RD

(Asphalt)

(Gravel)

TO
HOBACK JCT

GAME CREEK LOOP

Hike 14
South Park
Big Game Winter Range

Hiking Distance: 2.5 miles round trip
Hiking Time: 1.5 hours
Elevation Gain: Level hiking
Topo: U.S.G.S. Jackson

Summary of hike: This hike loops through a valley with mountain views in every direction. It crosses streams and strolls along the Snake River through a large stand of cottonwood trees. Picnic areas along the river are available.

This area is managed by the Wyoming Game and Fish Department. It provides the elk a winter range and feeding ground. During spring and summer it is a bird habitat for feeding, nesting, and raising young.

Driving directions: From downtown Jackson, drive 7 miles south on Highway 89. Turn right by the "South Park" sign. Drive one mile down into the valley, and park at the end of the road by the hay sheds and the bridge.

Hiking directions: Walk across the bridge and take the trail to the left past the log corral towards the cottonwood trees and the Snake River. At the river, take the trail to the right which leads alongside the Snake River and through the forest. A jeep trail loops back through a meadow towards the hay barns and parking area.

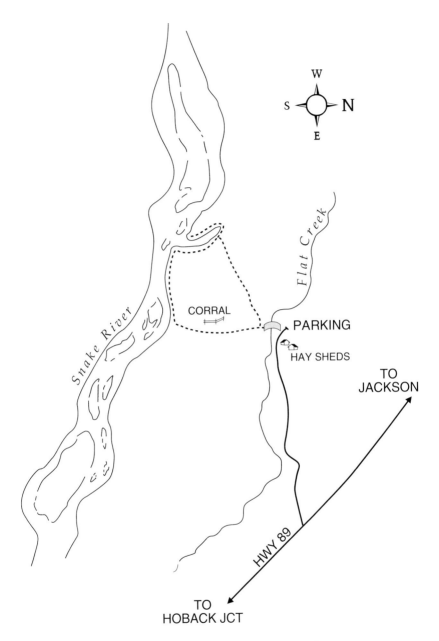

W

S   N

E

Flat Creek

Snake River

CORRAL

PARKING

HAY SHEDS

TO JACKSON

TO
HOBACK JCT

HWY 89

SOUTH PARK
BIG GAME WINTER RANGE

Hike 15
Dog Creek Trail

Hiking Distance: 4.5 miles round trip
Hiking Time: 2 hours
Elevation Gain: 300 feet
Topo: U.S.G.S. Munger Mountain

Summary of hike: Dog Creek Trail is in the Teton National Forest. This hike is like an arboretum of wildflowers. The trail follows a stream up the valley. Moose are frequently seen in this area.

Driving directions: From Jackson, drive south on Highway 89 for 14 miles to the Hoback Junction. Take the right fork at the junction, and drive 4.3 miles to the Wilson-Fall Creek Road. A sign marks this turn. Turn right, drive 1/4 mile, and park along the side of the road.

Hiking directions: Walk along the old jeep trail on the left (south) side, which intersects with the Wilson-Fall Creek Road. About 300 yards ahead, take the right trail, crossing a bridge over Dog Creek. Continue past the corrals to the trailhead. The trail follows the waters of Dog Creek to the left. The Dog Creek and Little Dog Creek junction is 2 1/4 miles from the trailhead. To the left is Dog Creek, and to the right is Little Dog Creek. The trail divides here. Each of these trails continues for many miles alongside both creeks. I turned back at the junction. To return, retrace your steps.

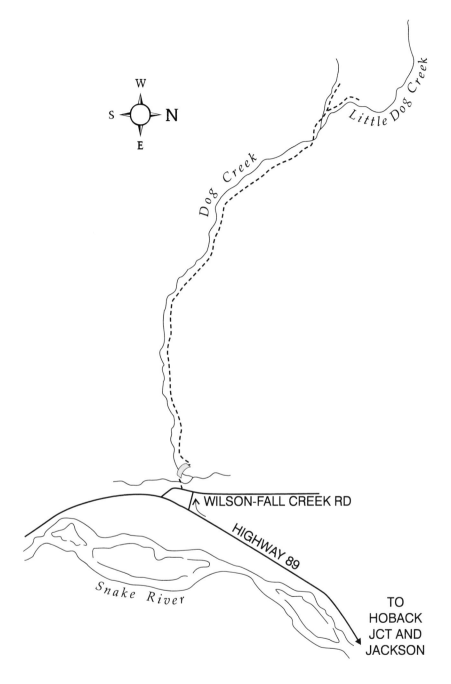

Little Dog Creek

Dog Creek

WILSON-FALL CREEK RD

HIGHWAY 89

Snake River

TO HOBACK JCT AND JACKSON

DOG CREEK TRAIL

Hike 16
Granite Falls and Hot Springs

Hiking Distance: 1 mile round trip
Hiking Time: 0.5 miles
Elevation Gain: 300 feet
Topo: U.S.G.S. Granite Falls and Crystal Peak

Summary of hike: This hike follows Granite Creek as it cascades to the magnificent Granite Falls (photo on back cover). Two very different and separate hot springs are accessible to soak in and swim .

Driving directions: From Jackson, drive south 14 miles on Highway 89 to the Hoback Junction. Take the left fork (Highway 191/189) towards Pinedale. Drive 11.5 miles to the Granite Recreational Area turnoff. A large sign marks the turn. Turn left and drive 10 miles on a gravel road to Granite Hot Springs. Park in the lot at the end of the road.

Hiking directions: Walk through the gate towards Granite Hot Springs. This wonderful hot springs, built in 1933, has a swimming pool and changing rooms. To head towards Granite Falls, take the right trail. As you hike, you will see the powerful Granite Creek swiftly tumbling towards the falls. Past the falls, a steep trail to the right descends down to the creek. There is another natural hot soaking pool 50 yards in front of the falls. To return, retrace your steps back to Granite Hot Springs.

Taking the left trail at the beginning of the hike leads through a beautiful forest into the canyon. Moose frequent the meadow which is just 15 minutes from the trailhead. This trail is part of a much longer trail to Turquoise Lake (10 miles) and Cache Creek (17 miles).

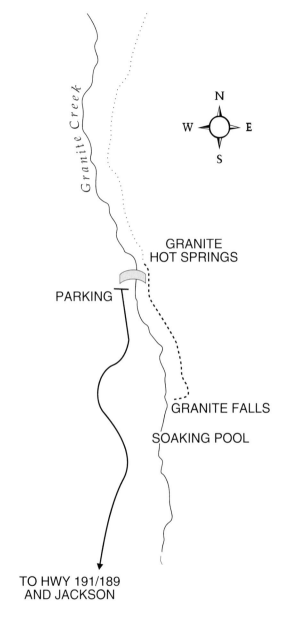

Granite Creek

GRANITE
HOT SPRINGS

PARKING

GRANITE FALLS

SOAKING POOL

TO HWY 191/189
AND JACKSON

GRANITE FALLS
AND HOT SPRINGS

NOTES

Information Sources

Grand Teton National Park
Moose Visitors Center
P.O. Drawer 170
Moose, WY 83012
(located at south entrance of
Grand Teton National Park)
(307) 733-2880

Jenny Lake Ranger Station
(307) 733-2880 Ext. 265

Wyoming State Visitors Center
532 N. Cache
Jackson, WY 83001
(307) 733-3316

Wyoming Dept. of Tourism
I-25 and College Drive
Cheyenne, WY 82002
(800) 225-5996

Jackson Hole Visitors Council
532 N. Cache
Jackson, WY 83001
(800) 782-0011

Jackson Hole Chamber of Commerce
P.O. Box E
Jackson, WY 83001
(307) 733-3316

Bridger-Teton National Forest
340 N. Cache
Jackson, WY 83001
(307) 739-5500

Bridger-Teton National Forest
Buffalo Ranger District
P.O. Box 278
Moran, WY 83013
(307) 543-2386

Grand Teton Lodge Co.
P.O. Box 240
Moran, WY 83013
(307) 543-2855

Jackson Ranger District
P.O. Box 1689
Jackson, WY 83001
(307) 733-4755

Targhee National Forest
Teton Basin Ranger District
Driggs, ID 83422
(208) 354-2431

Other Day Hike Guidebooks

___ Day Hikes on Oahu $6.95
___ Day Hikes on Maui 6.95
___ Day Hikes on Kauai 6.95
___ Day Trips on St. Martin 9.95
___ Day Hikes in Denver 6.95
___ Day Hikes in Boulder, Colorado 6.95
___ Day Hikes in Steamboat Springs, Colorado 6.95
___ Day Hikes in Summit County, Colorado
    Breckenridge, Dillon, Frisco, Keystone, and Silverthorne 6.95
___ Day Hikes in Aspen, Colorado 7.95
___ Day Hikes in Yellowstone National Park
    25 Favorite Hikes 7.95
___ Day Hikes in the Grand Tetons and Jackson Hole 7.95
___ Day Hikes in Los Angeles
    Venice/Santa Monica to Topanga Canyon 6.95
___ Day Hikes in the Beartooths
    Red Lodge to Cooke City, Montana 4.95

These books may be purchased at your local bookstore or they will be glad to order them. For a full list of titles available directly from ICS Books, call toll-free 1-800-541-7323. Visa or Mastercard accepted.

Please include $2.00 per order to cover postage and handling. Please send the books marked above. I enclose $_____

Name _____

Address _____

City _____ State _____ Zip _____

Credit Card # _____ Exp. _____

Signature_____

1-800-541-7323

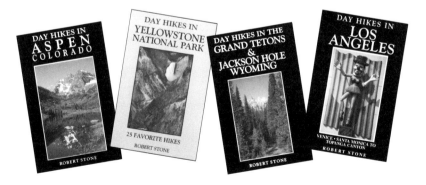

Distributed by:
ICS Books, Inc.
1370 E. 86th Place, Merrillville, In. 46410
1-800-541-7323 · Fax 1-800-336-8334

TOM EGENES

About the Author

The lure of the beautiful Rocky Mountains drew Robert to Red Lodge, Montana, in 1979. Hiking, horsepacking, and living in the Rockies has fulfilled a lifelong dream.

Robert Stone has traveled and photographed extensively throughout Asia, Europe, the Caribbean, Hawaii, and the Continental United States.